Celtic
Britain

Celtic Britain

Photographs by Janet and Colin Bord
Text by Nicholas Best

WEIDENFELD AND NICOLSON
LONDON

INTRODUCTION

*M*ID-EUROPEAN in origin, the Celts were a fair-haired, blue-eyed people who migrated to Britain at the end of the Bronze Age. They brought iron with them when they came, the most sophisticated metal of the day. It gave them an immeasurable advantage over the men of the Bronze Age, enabling the Celts to dominate all parts of Britain except perhaps the far north. When danger threatened, they built elaborate forts on hilltops, but for the rest of the time they lived in villages of round houses sunk into the earth. In the south, they built towns as well, with regular market places and a coinage that was sometimes gold but more often iron. By the time Julius Caesar invaded in 55 bc, they had established a civilization

far more sophisticated than anything the Romans had been expecting.

Their culture was subordinated to the Romans during the occupation, but they came into their own again after the invaders had left. By then they were converting to Christianity, abandoning the old Druid practices of human sacrifice in favour of the missionary teachings of the saints. The new religion was widely reflected in Celtic art, notably in sculptured crosses but finding its finest expression perhaps in the Lindisfarne Gospels. It was the Celts also who built the country's first monasteries and adopted the idea of marking the date from the birth of Christ.

Yet none of this protected them from the pagan forces which invaded the island during the Dark Ages. First the Anglo-Saxons overran them, then the Danes. The Celts withdrew in disarray to the mountain fastness of Wales and to the furthest reaches of Scotland, but even this was not enough to save them from the Normans. Their culture became irredeemably marginalized after the Conquest, although it survived for centuries and lives on in Wales to this day.

HEREFORDSHIRE BEACON

HEREFORD & WORCESTER

*T*HIS grassy rampart marks the site of a remarkable Iron Age fort covering 44 acres on top of the Malvern Hills.

The citadel was defended by an intricate network of trenches and fall-back positions, culminating in a thick stone wall 60 feet above the ditch.

JARLSHOF

SHETLAND

*N*AMED after the Norsemen who later settled here, the settlement has in fact been inhabited since Neolithic times. These 'wheel' houses date from the 3rd to the 8th century AD. Each has a series of individual rooms radiating outwards from a central hearth.

MAEN MADOC

POWYS

*N*INE feet high, this pillar stands beside the Roman road Sarn Helen. It has probably been there since 2000 BC. Some time between the 5th and 9th centuries AD, a Roman inscription was added, saying that it was the stone of Dervacus, son of Justus, who lies there.

THE WREKIN

O N a clear day, 17 counties can be seen from the top of the Wrekin. It was a prominent hillfort during the Iron Age and was useful again in 1588, when a fire was lit on the summit to give warning of the Spanish Armada.

GLASTONBURY TOR

SOMERSET

*L*EGEND has it that Joseph of Arimathea visited Glastonbury to bury the Holy Grail (the chalice used at the Last Supper) in the waters of a spring on the Tor. The church tower on the top dates from the 14th century, when Glastonbury was a popular place of pilgrimage.

TINTAGEL CASTLE

CORNWALL

*J*UTTING out towards Ireland, the Tintagel peninsula is traditionally thought to be the birthplace of King Arthur. A monastery built around AD 500 was abandoned after the Norman Conquest. The ruins here are of the Norman castle built on the site.

ST BRYNACH'S CROSS

DYFED

*N*EVERN church, in Dyfed, is dedicated to St Brynach, a 5th-century Irishman who spent his life in prayer nearby. St Brynach's Cross in the churchyard is 1,000 years old and 13 feet high, one of the best preserved Celtic crosses in Wales.

KING DONIERT'S STONE

CORNWALL

*T*HE stone stands near St Cleer in Cornwall. The badly weathered inscription reads, 'Doniert ordered... for... his soul'. It may refer to King Dungarth of Cornwall, drowned in 875.

IONA CATHEDRAL

IONA

*O*NLY 3 miles long, the island of Iona was the ancient burial place of Scottish kings. St Columba arrived in 563 to convert the natives to Christianity. The island's monastery was destroyed during the Reformation, but the ruins now belong to the Iona Cathedral Trust.

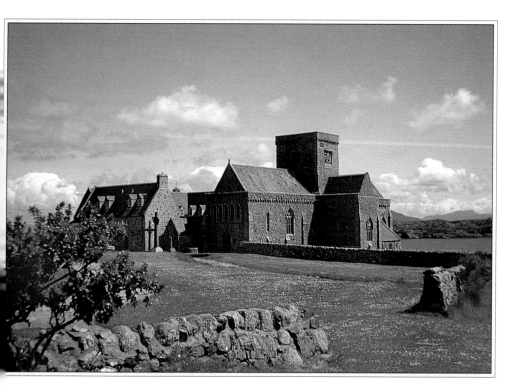

CHYSAUSTER

CORNWALL

*E*ngland's oldest village street dates from 100
BC. An Iron Age settlement in Cornwall,
it was inhabited by farmers and (perhaps)
tin miners, a civilized people who didn't
bother with fortifications but built terraced
gardens instead.

MAIDEN CASTLE

DORSET

ON a Dorset hilltop, Maiden Castle was a major fort in prehistoric times. The Romans stormed it around AD 43 and the Romano-British built a pagan temple there in the 4th century. In 1937 a mass grave was found near the eastern end, full of people killed by swords and arrows.

LLANTWIT MAJOR

SOUTH GLAMORGAN

*O*N the left of the picture, in the Old Church at Llantwit, stands the Cross of St Illtyd, dating from about AD 800. Now without its wheel cross, it was placed there, according to the Latin inscription, by one Samson 'for the good of his soul'.

ST GOVAN'S CHAPEL

DYFED

*M*UCH restored in the Middle Ages, the chapel was probably built soon after St Govan's death in 586. It marks the spot where the cliff reputedly opened to protect him from robbers. A hermit's cell was built on the site of the miracle and the saint spent the rest of his life there before being buried under the altar.

DUN CARLOWAY BROCH

WESTERN ISLES

$\mathcal{N}$o one knows for sure who built Scotland's brochs, although they seem to date from about 100 BC. This one, on the Lewis coast, shows the typical broch construction of a double wall with room for a gallery or stairway in between.

MOUSA BROCH

SHETLAND

A BROCH is a small Scottish fortress, probably dating from the Iron Age. This one, known as Moseyjarborg to the Norsemen, is the best preserved of the 500 built. It features as the scene of an elopement in the Orkneyinga Saga.

BARDSEY ISLAND

GWYNEDD

*K*NOWN also as the island of 20,000 saints, this was an important place of pilgrimage from the 5th century onwards. St Cadfan is said to have erected a monastery here in 429. Among the Welsh, three pilgrimages to Bardsey were reckoned to be the same as one to Rome.

ST NON'S CHAPEL

DYFED

*T*HIS is traditionally the birthplace of St David, patron saint of Wales, in the 6th century. The chapel, named after his mother, was built later. Its layout (north to south, rather than east to west) suggests that it is probably pre-Norman in origin.

———•••———

MEIFOD

POWYS

*M*EIFOD was the summer residence of the
princes of Powys. Nobody knows the exact
date of this grave slab in the church, but the
Norse and early Christian symbols suggest the
9th or 10th centuries at the latest.

CARN EUNY

CORNWALL

A FOGOU is a stone-lined underground chamber. This one, in Cornwall, is part of an Iron Age settlement that flourished long before the Roman invasion.

———◆◆◆———

EYAM

DERBYSHIRE

*T*HIS is a splendid example of a Celtic cross, either 8th or 9th century. It stands in a Derbyshire churchyard and is remarkable for still retaining its cross-head in near-perfect condition.

PENMACHNO MEMORIAL STONE

GWYNEDD

*C*ARVED with the sacred Chi-Rho (Christos) monogram, this memorial stone in Penmachno church dates from the 5th or 6th century. Its Latin inscription suggests that Roman influence survived long after the Romans themselves had left.

MOTE OF MARK

DUMFRIES AND GALLOWAY

*N*OT much remains of it now, but this was once an Iron Age fort, Scottish style, at Rockcliffe on the coast of Dumfries. Research suggests that it was still being used as a fort during the Dark Ages.

DINAS EMRYS

GWYNEDD

*A*CCORDING to legend, Vortigern, a 5th century King of Britain, tried to build a tower here, but was thwarted by 2 dragons sleeping in the pool below. When they awoke, the red dragon killed the white one, symbolizing Welsh victory over England and the eventual accession of Henry VII.

GARN FAWR

DYFED

*T*HIS ancient Welsh hillfort was built on Strumble Head, 600 feet above sea level. Whatever battles were fought there, none of them could have been more farcical than the last invasion of Britain in 1797. The French landed a force of convicts nearby - who promptly got drunk and surrendered.

ACKNOWLEDGEMENTS

Text © Weidenfeld & Nicolson 1995
Photographs © Janet and Colin Bord
Jacket photograph © Homer Sykes

First published in Great Britain in 1995 by George Weidenfeld & Nicolson Ltd
Orion House, 5 Upper St Martin's Lane, London WC2H 9EA

British Library Cataloguing-in-Publication Data
A catalogue record for this book is available from the British Library

Cover and series design by Peter Bridgewater/Bridgewater Book Company
House Editor: Beth Vaughan

Front cover: St Pirans Cross, Cornwall
Half-title illustration: Female exhibitionist carved on exterior of
Kilpeck church, Hereford & Worcester
Frontispiece: Celtic cross in Cardinham churchyard, Cornwall
Introduction: Ruined church, Llanddwyn Island Anglesey, Gwynedd